Apple Numbers for Beginners 2025

The Ultimate 7-Day Crash Course to Master Functions, Macros, and Formulas with Simple, Step-by-Step Instructions

Eric Techson

Copyright © 2024. **Eric Techson**

All rights reserved

No part of this publication may be reproduced, distributed, or transmitted in any form or by any means, including photocopying, recording, or other electronic or mechanical methods, without the prior written permission of the publisher, except in the case of brief quotations embodied in critical reviews and certain other noncommercial uses permitted by copyright law.

Table of Contents

Introduction 5

Chapter 1: Getting Started with Numbers 19

    Introduction to the Numbers Interface 19

Chapter 2: Functions Demystified 35

    What Are Functions? 35

    Basic Mathematical Functions 38

    Text and Date Functions 43

    Using Conditional Functions 47

  Practice Tasks 50

Chapter 3: Advanced Functions and Formulas 52

    Introduction to Complex Formulas 52

        How to Combine Functions into One Powerful Formula 53

        Lookup and Reference Functions 58

        Mathematical and Financial Functions 63

Chapter 4: Mastering Macros in Numbers 69

    What Are Macros and Why Should You Use Them? 69

Creating and Recording Your First Macro ... 71

Customizing Macros for Personal Use ... 73

Best Practices for Managing Macros

Chapter 5: Organizing and Analyzing Data in Numbers ... 84

Working with Tables and Charts ... 85

Introduction to Charts and How to Visually Represent Data ... 87

Sorting and Filtering Data ... 90

Using Filters to Manage and Analyze Data ... 92

Data Validation ... 95

Pivot Tables ... 97

Step-by-Step Guide to Creating Pivot Tables ... 98

Chapter 6: Time-Saving Tips and Tricks ... 102

Keyboard Shortcuts for Efficiency ... 103

How to Use Shortcuts to Streamline Your Workflow ... 105

Using Templates ... 106

Collaborating and Sharing Your Work ... 109

    Advanced Formatting Techniques   113
        Using Themes and Styles for a Polished Look   114

Chapter 7: Troubleshooting and Common Issues   119

    Common Problems and Their Solutions   120
        How to Troubleshoot Formatting and Display Issues   124
    Ensuring Accuracy   126
    Improving Performance   130

Conclusion   137

Appendices   151

Introduction

Welcome to the World of Numbers

Apple's Numbers app is an often-overlooked gem in the realm of spreadsheet applications. Unlike its counterparts, it's more than just a tool for organizing data—it's an intuitive, versatile platform that can significantly enhance your productivity, regardless of whether you're an individual, student, or professional. Whether you are working on personal projects, managing finances, or running a small business, mastering Numbers will allow you to navigate complex data effortlessly and present it in ways that are visually compelling and easy to understand. But as with any tool, the key to unlocking its full potential lies in understanding its functions, capabilities, and unique features.

If you've found yourself wondering about the nuances of Numbers and how it compares to other spreadsheet programs like Excel, you've come to the right place. In this book, you'll discover not just how to use Numbers, but how to use it like a pro. As you embark on this 7-day learning journey, you'll quickly see how Numbers' seamless integration with other Apple products, its powerful functions, and its intuitive user interface can make spreadsheet tasks simpler and even enjoyable.

Numbers for Beginners

While many users are familiar with basic spreadsheet tools, a surprising number are unaware of just how much Numbers can do—especially when it comes to its more advanced functions, macros, and formulas. For beginners, the initial introduction to Numbers can seem overwhelming. However, with the right guidance, even the most complex features can be broken down into bite-sized, manageable pieces. This book is designed specifically for those who may not be familiar with Numbers or other similar software. If you're transitioning from a different spreadsheet tool or simply looking to gain confidence in using Numbers, you will find that this guide is tailored to help you.

This book will walk you through every essential aspect of Numbers, providing the foundation you need to become proficient in the program. From understanding basic cell operations to applying advanced formulas and macros, we'll take it step by step, ensuring you never feel lost or overwhelmed. The goal is simple: by the end of this book, you'll be comfortable using Numbers and capable of performing everything from basic data entry to creating dynamic reports and automating tasks.

Why Mastering Numbers is Valuable for Everyday Users, Students, Professionals, and Small Businesses

Numbers is not just another spreadsheet tool—it is a comprehensive solution for anyone who works with data, regardless of their field. Mastering Numbers is incredibly valuable for several reasons, and it can empower you in ways you might not have imagined.

For everyday users, mastering Numbers can streamline routine tasks. It's perfect for managing personal finances, creating shopping lists, planning events, or keeping track of household budgets. With Numbers, all of these tasks become simpler, faster, and more organized. Whether you're planning your monthly expenses or keeping track of an ongoing project, Numbers helps you stay on top of it all.

For students, Numbers provides a powerful platform for organizing and presenting information. Whether you're creating reports, analyzing research data, or designing visually appealing presentations, Numbers can be used to make academic tasks more efficient. It's not just for data entry; it's for thinking critically about your data, visualizing trends, and communicating complex ideas in a clear, concise manner.

For professionals, mastering Numbers can significantly enhance your workflow. As someone who might regularly work with data, you'll find that Numbers has all the tools you need to analyze, present, and share your work effectively. With its ability to handle complex formulas, create professional-quality charts, and even automate repetitive tasks through macros, Numbers makes it easier to manage projects and tasks. Whether you're in finance, project management, marketing, or another field, the ability to use Numbers efficiently can boost your productivity and efficiency.

For small businesses, Numbers is a game-changer. While Excel is often seen as the industry standard for spreadsheets, Numbers offers an equally powerful, yet user-friendly, alternative. It is a fantastic tool for managing business budgets, creating invoices, tracking inventory, or managing employee data. Since Numbers integrates seamlessly with other Apple software, small businesses using Apple products can experience smooth collaboration and efficiency, helping them stay organized and focused on growth.

Ultimately, mastering Numbers isn't just about learning how to use the software—it's about unlocking a set of tools that will make managing and analyzing data easier, more intuitive, and more effective. Regardless of your background or profession, this book will teach you to leverage the full power of Numbers in a way that's accessible and meaningful to you.

What You Will Learn in This Book: Functions, Macros, Formulas, and Essential Tools

The heart of this book lies in the practical knowledge you'll gain. We won't just touch on the basics—we'll dive deep into the core functions, tools, and features that make Numbers stand out. Throughout this 7-day crash course, you will learn how to use Numbers in various contexts, from managing personal data to automating tasks at work.

Here's a closer look at what you'll be mastering:

1. **Functions**

   Functions are the building blocks of any spreadsheet. In Numbers, you can easily apply built-in functions to perform complex calculations quickly and efficiently. This book will teach you a wide range of functions, including the basic ones like SUM, AVERAGE, and COUNT, as well as more advanced functions for data analysis and manipulation. You'll learn how to apply these functions in a variety of real-life scenarios to streamline your workflow and improve your productivity.

2. **Formulas**

   While functions help you perform individual calculations, formulas allow you to combine them and create custom calculations. Throughout this book, you will discover how to create, modify, and troubleshoot formulas. From simple equations to more sophisticated calculations involving conditional logic and dynamic references, you'll gain the confidence to tackle any data challenge.

3. **Macros**

   If you've ever found yourself repeating the same task over and over in a spreadsheet, macros will be a game-changer. Macros automate repetitive actions, saving you time and effort. You'll learn how to record and create your own macros in Numbers, making it easy to automate everything from basic formatting tasks to complex calculations. By the end of this book, you'll have the skills to work faster and more efficiently.

4. **Essential Tools**

Numbers isn't just about formulas and macros; it's also packed with a range of tools that can make your data look great and function flawlessly. You'll learn how to create professional-looking charts, manage and sort large datasets, work with templates, and use advanced features like conditional formatting and data validation. These tools will help you stay organized, present data clearly, and avoid errors.

How to Use the 7-Day Structure to Maximize Learning

Learning Numbers doesn't have to be a daunting task. By breaking it down into manageable chunks, you can maximize your learning and make steady progress each day. This book is structured to help you master the core aspects of Numbers in just 7 days, without feeling rushed or overwhelmed.

Each day focuses on a specific aspect of Numbers, starting with the basics and gradually building up to more advanced features. By following the step-by-step instructions, you'll be able to practice and reinforce what you've learned. The 7-day format is designed to keep you on track, allowing you to build a solid understanding of Numbers in a short amount of time.

Throughout this book, you'll find plenty of examples, practice exercises, and tips to help you absorb the material. By the end of the week, you will be capable of confidently using Numbers for a wide range of tasks. You'll not only understand how to apply the functions, formulas, and macros you've learned, but you'll also have a deeper understanding of how to organize and present your data more effectively.

By the end of this book, you will have gained the skills necessary to navigate Numbers confidently and use it to streamline your workflow, whether you're managing personal projects, working on academic assignments, or boosting your productivity in the workplace. Each chapter will equip you with the tools, strategies, and knowledge you need to make the most of Numbers, and you'll be ready to tackle any challenge that comes your way.

Are you ready to begin? Let's get started and transform your understanding of Numbers!

Chapter 1: Getting Started with Numbers

Introduction to the Numbers Interface

When you first open Numbers, the world of spreadsheets opens up to you in a clean, intuitive workspace. Apple has designed the Numbers interface to be easy to navigate while providing all the necessary tools to help you manage your data effectively. If you're accustomed to other spreadsheet programs, you'll find that the Numbers interface has a unique layout, making it both fresh and user-friendly. Even if you've never used a spreadsheet before, this chapter will guide you through the basics of Numbers and give you a solid foundation to build your skills.

The **Numbers workspace** is divided into several key sections that you'll need to become familiar with. These sections include the toolbar, the main spreadsheet area, and the formula bar, each of which plays an important role in working efficiently with data.

1. **Toolbar**: Located at the top of the screen, the toolbar contains essential tools that you'll use frequently. It provides shortcuts for formatting options, inserting tables, adding shapes and images, and more. The toolbar is customizable, so you can add or remove icons based on the functions you use most often. The **Format** button, for example, allows you to adjust the appearance of cells, text, and

other elements within your spreadsheet.

2. **Menus**: Below the toolbar, the menus offer more detailed options that help you control the functionality of your document. These menus include options like **File**, **Edit**, **View**, **Insert**, and **Format**, each of which contains submenus with various tools you can use to manipulate your document. The **Insert** menu allows you to add things like tables, text boxes, charts, and images, while the **Format** menu lets you adjust the style and appearance of your data.

3. **Main Workspace**: The grid of cells is the heart of Numbers. This is where you'll input your data, create formulas, and apply functions. The grid is

arranged into rows and columns, and each intersection is a cell that can hold numbers, text, or other data types.

4. **Formula Bar**: The formula bar sits just below the toolbar and provides a space for entering and viewing formulas. When you click on a cell, any data or formula you enter appears in this bar, making it easy to edit and apply formulas.

Creating a New Spreadsheet and Navigating Between Sheets

Getting started with a new spreadsheet in Numbers is simple. To create a new document, click **File** in the top menu, then select **New**. You will be prompted to choose from a variety of templates. Numbers offers templates for a wide range of uses, including budgeting, invoicing, project tracking, and more. If you're starting from scratch, simply select a blank spreadsheet to create a new, empty document.

Once you've created your new spreadsheet, you'll likely need to navigate between sheets. Each Numbers document can contain multiple sheets, and you can switch between them with ease. At the top of the spreadsheet, you'll see a tab bar that displays the names of the sheets in your document. Clicking on a sheet name will switch the view to that particular sheet. You can add new sheets by clicking the + button on the left side of the tab bar, and you can rename or delete sheets by right-clicking on their tab and selecting the appropriate option.

Understanding how to move between sheets allows you to keep your document organized, especially when working on larger projects that require different datasets or sections. Additionally, you can use the **Sheet Navigator**, a small window that displays all the sheets in your workbook, making it easier to jump between different sections of your document.

Understanding the Basics

Once you're familiar with the interface and have created your new spreadsheet, it's time to start entering data and learning about the fundamental aspects of Numbers.

1. **Entering Data into Cells**: Cells are the building blocks of any Numbers document, and entering data

into them is a straightforward process. To enter data into a cell, simply click on it and start typing. You can enter a variety of data types, including numbers, text, dates, and even formulas. After typing the data, press **Enter** or **Return** to move to the next cell in the row, or **Tab** to move to the next cell in the column.

- **Numbers**: Enter numeric data to perform calculations or create tables.
- **Text**: You can input text in cells for labeling, descriptions, or as part of a data set.
- **Dates**: Numbers can automatically recognize and format dates, so when you type

something like "12/25/2025," it will format it as a date.
- **Formulas**: You can enter formulas into a cell by starting with an equal sign =, followed by the desired formula.

2. **Formatting Text, Numbers, and Dates**:

Numbers allows you to format your data to ensure it's displayed clearly and effectively. You can format text in cells by selecting the cell, and then choosing from the **Format** menu. You can change the font size, style, color, and alignment. To format numbers, you can change the number of decimal places, use currency symbols, or even display percentages. For dates, Numbers can automatically detect the date format and adjust it accordingly. You can customize the display of dates by choosing different date formats (e.g., "MM/DD/YYYY" or "Month Day, Year") from the formatting options.

3. **Working with Rows, Columns, and Tables**: A spreadsheet is composed of rows (which are horizontal) and columns (which are vertical). The intersection of rows and columns forms a cell. Numbers allows you to add, remove, and resize rows and columns with ease.

    - To **add a row or column**, simply right-click on the row number or column letter and choose **Insert Row** or **Insert Column**.

- To **delete a row or column**, right-click and select **Delete Row** or **Delete Column**.
- To **resize a row or column**, click and drag the edge of the row or column header to increase or decrease its size.

4. Tables in Numbers are incredibly versatile, and you can easily insert tables, merge cells, or split them depending on your needs. A table is a collection of rows and columns that organize data in a structured way. You can create multiple tables within a single sheet, making it easier to categorize and organize different types of information.

Basic Data Organization: Sorting and Filtering

Once you've entered your data, you'll likely want to organize it in a way that makes it easier to analyze and understand. Numbers provides a range of sorting and filtering options to help you manage your data effectively.

1. **Sorting**:

    Sorting allows you to arrange your data in a specific order, making it easier to spot trends and analyze information. You can sort data alphabetically, numerically, or by date. To sort a column, simply select the column header and choose either **Sort Ascending** or **Sort Descending** from the toolbar or the **Organize** menu. You can also sort by multiple columns to create a more refined order.

2. **Filtering**:

Filtering allows you to display only the data that meets certain criteria, making it easier to focus on the information that matters most. Numbers makes it easy to apply filters. To apply a filter, select the column you want to filter, click on the filter icon, and choose the criteria for the filter. You can filter by specific text, numbers, or even ranges of values. Filtering is particularly useful when working with large datasets, as it helps you quickly narrow down the data that you need to analyze.

Saving and Sharing Your Work

As you work on your Numbers spreadsheet, it's important to save your progress regularly and consider how you might want to share your work with others.

1. **File Formats and Saving Options**: Numbers allows you to save your work in different formats, making it easy to share your spreadsheets across platforms. By default, Numbers saves files in its own .numbers format, which retains all of the document's features and formatting. However, you may need to save your document in a different format, such as **Excel** or **PDF**, depending on who you're sharing it with. To save in a different format, go to the **File** menu and select **Export**

To. From there, you can choose Excel, PDF, or other formats.

2. **How to Collaborate and Share with Others**: One of the greatest advantages of using Numbers is its ability to collaborate seamlessly with others. Whether you're working on a project with colleagues or sharing data with a friend, Numbers makes it easy to work together in real time. To share a Numbers document, simply click the **Collaborate** button located in the toolbar. This will allow you to invite others to view or edit your document via **iCloud**. You can also choose to set permissions, such as view-only or edit access, ensuring that your collaborators have the appropriate level of access.

Numbers also integrates well with other Apple applications like **Pages** and **Keynote**, so you can create professional presentations or reports from your spreadsheet data with ease. Sharing your Numbers document is a simple process that allows you to work more efficiently and stay connected with your team.

This chapter has covered the basics of getting started with Numbers. With the information provided here, you should feel comfortable navigating the Numbers interface, entering and formatting data, organizing your work, and sharing your documents. As you continue to explore Numbers, you'll uncover more advanced features and begin to use them to streamline your workflow and enhance your productivity.

Chapter 2: Functions Demystified

What Are Functions?

In Numbers, functions are pre-programmed formulas designed to make calculations and data manipulation easier. A function is essentially a shortcut that performs a specific task, allowing you to save time and reduce the complexity of your work. Instead of manually entering complex calculations, you can use functions to automatically perform tasks such as adding up numbers, finding averages, or manipulating text and dates. Understanding how to use functions effectively is essential for unlocking the true potential of Numbers and becoming proficient in spreadsheet management.

Built-in functions in Numbers are diverse, ranging from basic mathematical operations to advanced conditional logic. They are grouped into categories such as mathematical functions, statistical functions, text manipulation functions, and date and time functions, among others. These functions allow you to simplify and automate tasks, making data management much more efficient.

Why Functions Are Crucial for Simplifying Calculations and Tasks

Functions in Numbers are vital because they simplify complex tasks, reduce the likelihood of errors, and increase the efficiency of your work. Without functions, performing even simple calculations could require hours of manual input and calculation. For example, if you wanted to sum up a large list of numbers, you'd have to add each value individually. But with the **SUM** function, you can instantly calculate the total of a range of cells, saving you both time and effort.

Moreover, functions allow for more accurate and dynamic calculations. When data changes, functions automatically recalculate the result, ensuring your calculations are always up to date. This is especially important when working with large datasets or performing tasks like budgeting or inventory tracking, where accurate and real-time calculations are crucial.

By learning how to use Numbers' functions, you'll be able to handle various tasks, from basic arithmetic to more complex data analysis, with ease and precision. Let's dive into some of the most commonly used functions in Numbers and explore how you can use them in practical scenarios.

Basic Mathematical Functions

Mathematical functions in Numbers are essential for performing quick calculations on numerical data. They allow you to summarize and analyze data without manually entering formulas. Here are some of the most commonly used basic mathematical functions:

SUM:

The **SUM** function is used to add up a range of numbers. For example, if you have a list of expenses in a column and want to find the total, you can use the SUM function. The syntax for the SUM function is simple:

scss

Copy code

=SUM(A1:A10)

1. This would add up all the values in cells A1 through A10.

    Practical Application: You can use the SUM function to track total sales for a month, add up expenditures in a budget, or calculate the overall score in a game or test.

AVERAGE:

The **AVERAGE** function calculates the

mean (average) of a range of numbers. It is useful when you need to find out the central tendency of a data set. The syntax is:

scss

Copy   code

=AVERAGE(A1:A10)

2. This function will give you the average of the values in cells A1 through A10. **Practical   Application**: If you're analyzing test scores or sales figures, you can use the AVERAGE function to find the average value, helping you understand trends or performance over time.

COUNT:

The **COUNT** function counts the number of cells in a range that contain numbers. It's useful when you want to determine how many entries are numeric within a specific dataset. The syntax is:

scss

Copy code

=COUNT(A1:A10)

3. This will count the number of cells in the range that contain numbers.
Practical Application: You can use the COUNT function to count how many transactions or sales occurred in a given period or to track how many products you have in stock.

MIN and MAX: The **MIN** and **MAX** functions are used to find the smallest and largest values in a range of numbers, respectively. These functions are helpful when you want to identify the extreme values in your data set. The syntax for each is:

scss

Copy code

=MIN(A1:A10)

=MAX(A1:A10)

4. These will return the lowest and highest values in the range of cells from A1 to A10.

Practical Application: The MIN function could be used to identify the least expensive item in a shopping list, while the MAX function might help you find the highest score in a series of tests.

Text and Date Functions

In addition to mathematical functions, Numbers provides a range of functions to manipulate text and date data. These functions are essential for organizing, sorting, and analyzing non-numeric data.

CONCATENATE:

The **CONCATENATE** function combines multiple text strings into one. It is commonly used when you want to merge first and last names, addresses, or other sets of data into a single column. The syntax is:

scss

Copy code

```
=CONCATENATE(A1, " ", B1)
```

1. This function combines the text in cell A1 and cell B1, with a space between

them.

Practical Application: Use this function when creating full names from first and last names or when combining various data fields into one string.

LEFT and **RIGHT**: The **LEFT** and **RIGHT** functions allow you to extract a specific number of characters from the beginning or end of a text string. The syntax for LEFT is:

scss

Copy code

=LEFT(A1, 3)

This extracts the first three characters from the text in cell A1. Similarly, the RIGHT function works the same way but from the end of the string.

scss

Copy code

=RIGHT(A1, 4)

2. **Practical Application**: You can use the LEFT function to extract area codes from phone numbers or the first part of an email address. The RIGHT function is helpful when extracting the last part of an email or a product code.

TODAY:

The **TODAY** function returns the current date. This is particularly useful for creating time-sensitive documents, such as tracking deadlines or calculating the difference between two dates. The syntax is simply:

scss

Copy code
=TODAY()

3. **Practical Application**: Use the TODAY function to automatically insert the current date into your spreadsheet, making it easier to track progress over time.

DATE:

The **DATE** function allows you to create a date value by specifying the year, month, and day. The syntax is:

scss
Copy code
=DATE(2025, 12, 25)

4. This function will return the date December 25, 2025.

Practical Application:

The DATE function is useful when you need to create dates dynamically or when working with schedules and deadlines.

Using Conditional Functions

Conditional functions are powerful tools that allow you to perform actions based on specific criteria. These functions are often used for decision-making within spreadsheets. Here are three essential conditional functions in Numbers:

IF:

The **IF** function allows you to perform a test on data and return one value if the test is true, and another value if it is false. The syntax is:

arduino

Copy code

=IF(A1 > 100, "Above 100", "Below 100")

1. This function checks if the value in cell A1 is greater than 100. If it is, it returns "Above 100"; otherwise, it returns "Below 100."

   Practical Application: Use the IF function for decision-making scenarios, such as grading systems or conditional discounts.

COUNTIF:

The **COUNTIF** function counts the number of cells in a range that meet a specific condition. The syntax is:

less

Copy code

=COUNTIF(A1:A10, ">100")

2. This will count the number of cells in the range A1 to A10 that contain values greater than 100.

Practical Application: COUNTIF is helpful for counting entries that meet certain criteria, such as counting how many sales transactions exceed a certain amount.

SUMIF:

The **SUMIF** function sums the values in a range that meet a specific condition. The syntax is:

less
Copy code
=SUMIF(A1:A10, ">100")

3. This will add up all the values in the range A1 to A10 that are greater than 100.

Practical Application: Use SUMIF to calculate total sales over a specific value or sum up expenses for particular categories.

Practice Tasks

To solidify your understanding of these basic functions, try the following practice tasks:

1. **Create a budget spreadsheet**: Use the SUM, AVERAGE, MIN, and MAX functions to track your income and expenses over a month. Create categories for different types of expenses and calculate the total expenditure and average spending per category.

2. **Text manipulation**: Use the CONCATENATE, LEFT, RIGHT, and DATE functions to combine and manipulate data such as names, dates, and addresses.

3. **Conditional tasks**: Build a spreadsheet that tracks employee performance or student grades. Use IF, COUNTIF, and SUMIF to create a conditional grading system or performance analysis.

These hands-on exercises will help reinforce the skills you've learned and provide practical experience with the most commonly used functions in Numbers.

Chapter 3: Advanced Functions and Formulas

Introduction to Complex Formulas

As you become more comfortable with the basic functions in Numbers, it's time to explore more advanced formulas that will allow you to perform complex calculations and automate even more aspects of your spreadsheets. Complex formulas are often combinations of multiple functions working together to achieve a specific result. By combining functions, you can build powerful and dynamic formulas that streamline your tasks and increase efficiency. Whether you're calculating business projections, managing finances, or analyzing large datasets, mastering advanced formulas will unlock new levels of productivity and precision.

In this chapter, we will explore how to combine different functions into complex formulas, the best practices for formula syntax, and how these formulas can be applied to real-world business and personal scenarios.

How to Combine Functions into One Powerful Formula

Combining functions into a single formula allows you to perform multiple tasks in one step. For example, you could use a combination of mathematical, logical, and text functions to analyze a dataset and return a customized result. When combining functions, it's important to follow proper syntax and structure to ensure that the formula works correctly. Here's an example of how functions can be combined in Numbers:

Suppose you have a sales dataset and you want to calculate the bonus for each employee based on their sales performance. The bonus is calculated as 10% of the sales if the sales amount is greater than $1,000, otherwise, there is no bonus. You can use the **IF** function combined with multiplication to achieve this:

scss
Copy code
=IF(A2 > 1000, A2 * 0.1, 0)

In this example:

- **A2** is the cell containing the sales figure.
- The **IF** function checks if the sales amount is greater than 1,000.
- If the condition is true, it multiplies the sales amount by 10% (0.1).
- If the condition is false, it returns 0 (no bonus).

This formula combines logic and mathematical operations to deliver a result based on the conditions specified. As you get more advanced, you will combine even more functions for more intricate calculations.

Formula Syntax and Best Practices

Understanding formula syntax is crucial when combining functions. Here are some key points to remember for writing effective formulas:

Use parentheses correctly: Functions and operations should be enclosed in parentheses to ensure the correct order of operations. For instance, in a formula like:

scss

Copy   code

=(A1 + A2) * B1

1. The addition of **A1 + A2** is performed first, followed by multiplication by **B1**.
2. **Start formulas with an equals sign**:
   Every formula in Numbers begins with an equals sign (=). Without it, the

program will interpret the entry as plain text rather than a formula.

Separate functions with commas: When combining multiple functions, separate them with commas. For example:
less

Copy code

=IF(A1 > 1000, VLOOKUP(A1, B1:B10, 1, FALSE), 0)

3. This formula combines an **IF** function with a **VLOOKUP** function to return a value from a table only if a specific condition is met.
4. **Avoid errors by checking your references**:
Ensure that all cell references are correct. When working with large datasets, double-check your cell ranges

to avoid errors that could affect your calculations.

By following these basic rules and practices, you'll be able to craft complex formulas that perform multiple tasks in one go.

Lookup and Reference Functions

Lookup and reference functions are invaluable tools in Numbers, especially when you need to search for specific data in large datasets. These functions allow you to retrieve information from other cells, tables, or ranges based on specific criteria, making it easier to work with large amounts of data.

VLOOKUP:

The **VLOOKUP** (vertical lookup) function is

used to search for a value in the first column of a range and return a corresponding value from another column. For example, if you have a list of employees and their salaries, you can use VLOOKUP to find the salary of a specific employee.

The syntax for **VLOOKUP** is:

scss

Copy code

=VLOOKUP(lookup_value, table_array, col_index_num, [range_lookup])

Example:

php

Copy code

=VLOOKUP("John Doe", A2:B10, 2, FALSE)

1. In this example:
    - **"John Doe"** is the lookup value.

- **A2:B10** is the table array where the employee names are in column A and salaries in column B.
- **2** indicates that the salary is in the second column of the table.
- **FALSE** means an exact match is required.

2. **Practical Application**: Use VLOOKUP to find employee data, look up product prices, or search for customer information in a large database.

HLOOKUP:

The **HLOOKUP** function works similarly to VLOOKUP but searches for the lookup value in the first row of a table, returning a corresponding value from a specified row beneath it. The syntax is:

scss

Copy code

=HLOOKUP(lookup_value, table_array, row_index_num, [range_lookup])

3. **Practical Application**: HLOOKUP is useful when your data is organized horizontally instead of vertically. It can be used to search for information in budgets, inventory lists, or financial reports.

INDEX and MATCH: The **INDEX** and **MATCH** functions work together to perform more flexible lookups than VLOOKUP or HLOOKUP. **INDEX** returns a value from a specified range based on row and column numbers, while **MATCH** finds the position of a value within a range.

The combined syntax for INDEX and MATCH is:

scss

Copy   code

=INDEX(return_range, MATCH(lookup_value, lookup_range, 0))

Example:

less

Copy   code

=INDEX(B2:B10, MATCH("John Doe", A2:A10, 0))

4. In this example:
    - **MATCH** finds the row number where "John Doe" appears in column A.
    - **INDEX** then returns the corresponding value from

column B (e.g., John Doe's salary).

5. **Practical Application**: INDEX and MATCH are more powerful than VLOOKUP and HLOOKUP when you need to look up data in any direction and retrieve more dynamic results. They are commonly used in financial modeling and data analysis tasks.

Mathematical and Financial Functions

As you delve deeper into Numbers, you'll encounter advanced mathematical and financial functions that are essential for calculations in professional settings, especially for budgeting, forecasting, and loan management.

ROUND:

The **ROUND** function rounds a number to a specified number of digits. For example, you may want to round your financial figures to two decimal places for consistency. The syntax is:

scss

Copy code

=ROUND(A1, 2)

1. This will round the value in cell A1 to two decimal places.
Practical Application: Use the ROUND function when you need to standardize figures, such as when dealing with currency or measurements.

SQRT:

The **SQRT** function calculates the square root of a number. The syntax is:

scss

Copy code

=SQRT(A1)

2. This function is useful in mathematical calculations and financial modeling.
   Practical Application: Use SQRT when calculating things like loan amortization or other formulas that require square roots.

PMT:

The **PMT** function is used to calculate the payment amount for a loan based on constant payments and a fixed interest rate. The syntax is:

scss

Copy code

=PMT(interest_rate, number_of_periods, loan_amount)

3. **Practical Application**: Use the PMT function to calculate monthly mortgage payments, car loans, or personal loan repayments.

Practice Tasks

To strengthen your understanding of advanced functions and formulas, try these practice exercises:

1. **Loan Calculation**: Use the PMT function to calculate monthly payments for a loan. Assume you have a loan amount of $20,000

with an annual interest rate of 5% over 5 years.

2. **Business Budget Forecast**: Use a combination of VLOOKUP, INDEX, and MATCH to pull data from a financial dataset and forecast next quarter's revenue based on sales trends.

3. **Sales Performance Report**: Build a report that calculates employee bonuses based on sales performance. Use IF, VLOOKUP, and SUMIF to calculate bonus percentages, commission amounts, and total earnings.

By completing these tasks, you will gain hands-on experience in using advanced functions and formulas, helping you become more efficient and skilled in managing complex data in Numbers.

Chapter 4: Mastering Macros in Numbers

What Are Macros and Why Should You Use Them?

In the world of spreadsheets, tasks can often become repetitive, especially when you are working with large datasets, frequently updating reports, or performing the same sequence of actions over and over again. This is where **macros** come into play. Macros are automation tools that allow you to record and repeat a set of actions in Numbers, saving you time and reducing the possibility of human error.

A **macro** is essentially a shortcut to a series of commands or actions. By recording a macro, you can automate repetitive tasks such as formatting cells, applying formulas, or updating data. Once a macro is created, you can run it with just a click, eliminating the need to manually perform the same steps each time.

Using macros in Numbers not only enhances efficiency but also ensures consistency in your work. If you find yourself performing the same steps every day, automating the process with macros will free up time for more important tasks and reduce the chance of making mistakes.

In this chapter, we will explore the fundamentals of macros in Numbers, how to create and customize them, and how to apply them to real-world tasks like data analysis and reporting. Additionally, we'll cover best practices for managing macros effectively.

Creating and Recording Your First Macro

Getting started with macros is easier than you might think. Numbers allows you to create and record macros to automate many of your daily tasks. To help you understand how macros work, let's walk through a simple process of recording your first macro.

Step 1: Enabling Macros

Before you can start recording macros, you need to make sure that macros are enabled in Numbers. To do this, navigate to **Preferences** in Numbers and ensure that the **Macros** feature is turned on. Once enabled, you'll be able to access the macro recording tools.

Step 2: Recording a Macro

1. Open a new or existing spreadsheet in Numbers where you want to use the macro.
2. From the top menu, go to **Tools** and select **Record Macro**. This will begin the macro recording session.
3. Perform the actions you want to automate. For example, if you want to format a table, you might:
    - Highlight a range of cells.
    - Apply a specific font style or size.
    - Add borders or change the background color.

4. After you've completed your actions, click the **Stop Recording** button. Numbers will now store the steps you took as a macro.

Step 3: Naming and Saving Your Macro

After recording your macro, you'll be prompted to give it a name. Choose a descriptive name that will help you identify the macro later. You can also assign a shortcut key for quicker access to the macro in the future.

Customizing Macros for Personal Use

Once you've recorded a basic macro, you may want to customize it to suit your specific needs. Numbers allows you to edit and fine-tune your macros after they have been created. You can modify existing macros, adjust the order of operations, or add new steps to the process.

For example, if you recorded a macro to apply certain formatting to a table, but you now want to include additional data validation steps (like setting limits on cell inputs), you can edit the macro to incorporate these changes. Customizing macros ensures that they continue to meet your evolving needs.

Editing a Macro:

1. Go to the **Macros** section in the Numbers preferences.

2. Locate the macro you wish to edit and click on it.
3. Modify the actions or steps included in the macro.
4. Save your changes and assign the updated macro a new name, if desired.

Customizing your macros allows you to build a library of tailored actions that streamline your workflow and make your work more efficient.

Using Macros for Data Analysis

Macros become incredibly powerful when used for tasks like data analysis. If you often need to analyze large sets of data, perform calculations, or generate reports, macros can automate these processes, saving you time and effort.

Automating Data Entry:

If you're working with datasets that require frequent updates (e.g., sales data, inventory lists, etc.), a macro can automate data entry. For instance, you could create a macro that enters specific data into designated cells, applies necessary formatting, and even creates summary tables for analysis. Once the macro is set up, you can simply run it to quickly populate your spreadsheet with data.

Automating Calculations:

Suppose you are working with monthly financial data and you need to calculate totals, averages, and percentages for each department. Instead of manually performing these calculations each time, you can create a macro that does the job for you. For example:

- The macro could sum up sales figures for each department.
- It could calculate the average sales per month.
- It could also generate a report comparing this month's performance with the previous month.

By automating these tasks, you can spend less time on manual calculations and more time analyzing the results.

Automating Reports:

Another great use for macros in data analysis is automating the process of generating reports. If you need to create a weekly or monthly report, a macro can help. Once you've set up your report template (with necessary formatting, charts, and calculations), you can record a macro that automatically updates the report with the latest data each time you run it. This will save you significant time and reduce the risk of errors.

Best Practices for Managing Macros

As you start creating multiple macros, it's important to manage them efficiently to ensure that they are easy to access, edit, and organize. Here are some best practices to help you keep your macros under control:

1. **Naming Macros Clearly**: Give your macros descriptive names that explain their function. For example, instead of

naming a macro "Macro1," name it something more specific, like "Sales Data Formatter" or "Quarterly Report Generator." This will help you quickly identify the macro you need.

2. **Organizing Macros**: If you create many macros, consider organizing them into categories based on their function. For instance, you could have categories like "Data Entry Macros," "Financial Report Macros," and "Formatting Macros." This will make it easier to locate and run the macros when needed.

3. **Running Multiple Macros**: If you need to run multiple macros in sequence, you can set them up to be triggered automatically one after the other. Some tools in Numbers allow

you to group multiple macros together, creating a streamlined process for executing a series of tasks.

4. **Editing and Troubleshooting Macros**: Occasionally, a macro may not work as expected due to changes in your spreadsheet or new requirements. To troubleshoot, go back to the macro editor and review the steps to see if any updates are needed. You can add, remove, or reorder actions as necessary. If you encounter issues, check the actions for any errors or inconsistencies, and make adjustments accordingly.

5. **Documenting Macros**: To ensure that you or others can understand and maintain your macros in the future, document each one. Include details on

what the macro does, any special instructions, and what to do if problems arise. This documentation will be especially helpful if you're working in a team or sharing macros with others.

Practice Tasks

To master the art of macros, try creating a few of your own. Here are some exercises to help you practice and get comfortable with using macros in Numbers:

1. **Data Entry Automation**: Create a macro that enters a set of data (e.g., sales transactions) into a table. Include a step that automatically formats the table for readability.

2. **Financial Report Generator**: Build a macro that generates a quarterly financial report, complete with calculations for total revenue, expenses, and profit. The macro should apply formatting to the report and create a simple summary chart.
3. **Data Validation**: Record a macro that sets up data validation rules for a range of cells, ensuring that only certain values can be entered. This will help prevent errors in data entry.
4. **Repetitive Formatting**: Create a macro that formats text and numbers in a consistent style, such as bolding column headers, centering data, and applying currency formatting to financial figures.

By mastering macros, you will unlock a new level of productivity in Numbers. With the ability to automate repetitive tasks, streamline data analysis, and improve accuracy, macros are a valuable tool that can save you hours of work and reduce the chance of mistakes. Keep practicing and refining your skills, and you'll soon be able to tackle even the most complex tasks with ease.

Chapter 5: Organizing and Analyzing Data in Numbers

When working with data in Numbers, it's not just about entering numbers and performing calculations. Organizing and analyzing data effectively is key to unlocking its full potential. This chapter will guide you through the essential techniques and tools in Numbers, including tables, charts, sorting, filtering, data validation, and pivot tables. Whether you are a student, professional, or business owner, mastering these techniques will allow you to work more efficiently, make data-driven decisions, and create insightful reports.

Working with Tables and Charts

How to Create Tables and Organize Data

Tables are the foundation of data entry and organization in Numbers. When starting a new spreadsheet, one of the first things you'll need to do is create a table to store and structure your data. In Numbers, tables are highly customizable, making them ideal for different types of datasets—whether you're tracking sales, expenses, inventory, or project progress.

Creating a Table:

1. Open a new or existing spreadsheet in Numbers.

2. Click on the **Table** icon from the toolbar, and select the style of table you prefer. You can choose from a simple table, a list, or even pre-designed templates that offer advanced formatting.
3. Add columns and rows as needed. You can also adjust the column width and row height by dragging the borders.
4. Label your columns with clear, descriptive headings. For example, if you are tracking sales, columns might include **Product Name**, **Sales Volume**, **Price**, and **Date of Sale**.

Once your table is created, you can begin entering data. Numbers also provides tools for formatting, such as adjusting text size, changing cell colors, and applying currency or date formats to ensure your table is organized and easy to read.

Organizing Data in Tables: To keep your data organized, it's important to use consistent formatting and group related data together. For example:

- Use **bold headers** to differentiate column names.
- **Freeze the header row** so that it remains visible when scrolling through large datasets.
- **Use alternating row colors** to make reading across rows easier.

Introduction to Charts and How to Visually Represent Data

Charts are a powerful way to visualize your data and communicate trends or insights clearly. Numbers offers a range of chart types, including bar charts, line charts, pie charts, and scatter plots. Using charts helps to transform raw numbers into visually appealing and understandable information.

Creating a Chart:

1. Select the data you want to visualize in your table. For example, if you're tracking sales by month, select the **Date** and **Sales Volume** columns.
2. Click on the **Chart** icon in the toolbar and choose the type of chart that best represents your data.
3. Numbers will automatically generate a chart based on the selected data. You can further customize the chart's

appearance by adjusting colors, labels, axis titles, and adding data markers.
4. You can also create dynamic charts that update automatically as the data in your table changes.

Types of Charts:

- **Bar Charts**: Best for comparing categories, such as sales across different regions.
- **Line Charts**: Ideal for showing trends over time, such as sales performance across several months.
- **Pie Charts**: Perfect for illustrating proportions, such as the market share of different products.
- **Scatter Plots**: Useful for showing the relationship between two variables, such as price and sales volume.

By mastering charts, you can easily turn your data into insights that are easier to interpret and share with others.

Sorting and Filtering Data

Best Practices for Sorting Large Datasets

Sorting is one of the simplest yet most powerful techniques for organizing data in Numbers. Whether you are working with a small dataset or a large one, sorting allows you to arrange your data in a meaningful order, making it easier to spot patterns and draw conclusions.

How to Sort Data:

1. Select the column you want to sort by. If you want to sort by multiple columns

(for example, by **Date of Sale** and then by **Sales Volume**), hold down the **Command** key while selecting multiple columns.
2. Click the **Sort** button in the toolbar, and choose whether to sort in ascending or descending order. For example, sorting by **Date** in ascending order will arrange your data from the oldest to the most recent date.
3. You can also sort text columns alphabetically, numeric columns from lowest to highest, or dates in chronological order.

Sorting Best Practices:

- Always make sure to sort based on relevant columns that will help you understand the data better. For

instance, if you're tracking expenses, you might sort by **Category** or **Amount**.
- When sorting multiple columns, ensure the order makes sense for your analysis. Sorting by **Date** first, followed by **Sales Volume**, might help you observe sales trends over time.

Sorting large datasets can be time-consuming, but it's essential for organizing your data in a way that makes it easier to find insights and perform analysis.

Using Filters to Manage and Analyze Data

Filters allow you to display only the data that is relevant to your analysis, while hiding the rest. This is especially useful when working with large datasets where you need to focus on a specific subset of data, such as sales for a particular region or data from a specific date range.

How to Apply Filters:

1. Select the data range or table you want to filter.
2. Click the **Filter** icon in the toolbar.
3. Choose the column you want to filter by. For example, you could filter by **Product Category** to view only data for a specific product type.
4. Set criteria for your filter. For example, you might filter for **sales greater**

than **$100** or **dates within the last month**.

5. Once the filter is applied, only the rows that meet your criteria will be visible, allowing you to focus on relevant data.

Using Multiple Filters: You can also apply multiple filters simultaneously. For instance, you might filter by **Region** and **Sales Volume**, allowing you to analyze specific segments of your dataset.

Filter Best Practices:

- Use filters when you need to narrow down large datasets and focus on specific information.
- Remove filters after use to return to the full dataset and continue working.

Data Validation

Introduction to Data Validation Rules

Data validation is a crucial tool that ensures the accuracy and consistency of the data entered into your spreadsheet. By setting up validation rules, you can restrict the type of data entered into cells, such as only allowing numbers or dates, or creating dropdown lists for users to choose from.

How to Set Up Data Validation:

1. Select the range of cells where you want to apply data validation.
2. Go to the **Format** menu and click on **Cell**.
3. In the **Data Format** tab, select the type of validation you want. For

example, you can choose **Date**, **Number**, or **List**.

4. If you choose **List**, you can enter predefined values for a dropdown list. For instance, you could create a list of **Regions** like "North," "South," and "East" for users to select from.

Using Drop-Down Lists and Restrictions: Dropdown lists are useful for ensuring that users can only select from predefined options. For example, if you are tracking sales regions, you could create a dropdown list with the names of different regions, ensuring consistency in data entry.

Setting Restrictions: You can also set restrictions for numeric data. For example, if you are tracking product quantities, you might set a restriction that only numbers greater than 0 can be entered.

Pivot Tables

What Are Pivot Tables, and How to Use Them for Summarizing Large Datasets

Pivot tables are powerful tools used to summarize, analyze, and explore large datasets. With pivot tables, you can quickly rearrange your data to view it from different perspectives, making it easier to uncover trends and insights.

What Pivot Tables Can Do:

- **Summarize Data:** Pivot tables allow you to group data by categories and

aggregate information (e.g., sum of sales, average quantity sold).
- **Analyze Trends:** You can analyze data over time, by region, or by any other category.
- **Generate Reports:** Pivot tables are often used to create summarized reports that highlight key metrics.

Step-by-Step Guide to Creating Pivot Tables

1. **Select the Data:** Start by selecting the dataset you want to analyze.
2. **Insert Pivot Table:** Click on **Insert** in the menu bar and select **Pivot Table**.
3. **Configure the Pivot Table:** Drag and drop fields into the **Rows**, **Columns**, and **Values** sections. For

example, drag **Product Category** to the **Rows** section and **Sales Volume** to the **Values** section.

4. **Refining the Pivot Table:** You can further refine the pivot table by adding filters, sorting data, and changing how values are displayed (e.g., as sums, averages, etc.).

Pivot tables are a game-changer for analyzing large datasets, and they allow you to view your data in dynamic and flexible ways.

Practice Tasks

To help solidify your understanding of organizing and analyzing data in Numbers, try these practice tasks:

1. **Create a Table and Organize Data:**
   Build a table to track personal expenses or sales data. Include columns for date, category, amount, and description.
2. **Create a Chart:**
   Select your data and create a chart that visually represents your findings. For instance, create a bar chart to show the sales by product category.
3. **Apply Filters:**
   Filter a dataset to show only data for a particular category or date range, and observe how the results change.
4. **Create a Pivot Table:**
   Using a dataset with multiple columns, create a pivot table to summarize sales data by region and product category.

By mastering the techniques of organizing and analyzing data in Numbers, you will be able to turn complex datasets into actionable insights. Whether you are sorting data, creating charts, applying filters, or using pivot tables, these skills will make you more efficient and effective in your work. Keep practicing, and soon you'll be using these tools effortlessly to manage, analyze, and present data in Numbers.

Chapter 6: Time-Saving Tips and Tricks

When it comes to working with spreadsheets, efficiency is key. The faster and more smoothly you can navigate through your data, the more time you can save to focus on analysis and decision-making. In this chapter, we will explore several time-saving tips and tricks to help you become a Numbers pro. From keyboard shortcuts and templates to collaboration features and advanced formatting, these techniques will streamline your workflow and make your Numbers experience even more productive.

Keyboard Shortcuts for Efficiency

A List of Essential Shortcuts to Navigate Numbers Faster

Using keyboard shortcuts is one of the quickest ways to navigate and work in Numbers. Whether you're entering data, formatting cells, or moving between sheets, mastering shortcuts can save you valuable time and reduce the number of clicks you need to make.

Here are some essential keyboard shortcuts for Numbers:

- **Cmd + N**: Create a new spreadsheet.
- **Cmd + O**: Open an existing file.
- **Cmd + S**: Save your spreadsheet.

- **Cmd + Z**: Undo your last action.
- **Cmd + Shift + Z**: Redo your last undone action.
- **Cmd + C**: Copy selected data.
- **Cmd + V**: Paste copied data.
- **Cmd + X**: Cut selected data.
- **Cmd + Shift + K**: Insert a new row.
- **Cmd + Shift + L**: Insert a new column.
- **Cmd + F**: Find data in your sheet.
- **Cmd + A**: Select all cells.
- **Cmd + Shift + T**: Add a new table.
- **Cmd + B**: Bold selected text.
- **Cmd + I**: Italicize selected text.
- **Cmd + U**: Underline selected text.

By memorizing these basic shortcuts, you can perform tasks like copying, pasting, and navigating through cells faster, allowing you to work with greater efficiency.

How to Use Shortcuts to Streamline Your Workflow

In addition to the shortcuts listed above, you can use combinations of shortcuts to streamline more complex tasks. For example, instead of clicking through multiple menus to format your data, you can use **Cmd + B** to quickly bold text or **Cmd + 1** to open the formatting sidebar. By learning and incorporating these shortcuts into your routine, you'll notice a significant improvement in your speed and accuracy.

Furthermore, Numbers allows you to create custom shortcuts for actions that are important to your workflow. For example, if you frequently use a particular function or menu option, you can create a custom shortcut that eliminates the need to navigate through multiple tabs and options.

Using Templates

How to Use Pre-Made Templates for Budgeting, Schedules, and More

Templates are a great way to jumpstart your spreadsheet projects without having to create everything from scratch. Numbers offers a variety of pre-made templates that cover a wide range of needs, from budgeting and project management to invoices and schedules. Using templates can save you time, especially for tasks that require specific formatting and calculations.

How to Access and Use Templates:

1. Open Numbers and click on **File** in the top menu bar.
2. Select **New** to open the template gallery.
3. Browse through the available templates by category—budgeting, calendars, to-do lists, and more.
4. Once you find the template that fits your needs, click on it to open a new file based on that template.
5. You can then edit the data and customize the template to suit your personal or business needs.

Customizing Templates to Fit Personal Needs

While pre-made templates can give you a head start, you may find that you need to customize them to fit your specific requirements. Numbers allows you to modify almost any aspect of a template, from the structure of the table to the formatting and layout.

Customizing Templates:

- **Add or Remove Columns:** If a template includes columns that aren't relevant to your task, simply delete them. Alternatively, you can add new columns if additional information is needed.
- **Modify Formulas:** Templates often come with pre-built formulas to handle calculations like totals, averages, or percentages. You can edit these

formulas to suit your needs by clicking on the formula bar and making adjustments.

- **Change the Style:** You can change the colors, fonts, and borders in a template to match your personal style or the branding of your business.

Customizing templates is a simple and effective way to save time when working on recurring projects, ensuring that every new document follows a consistent format.

Collaborating and Sharing Your Work

Best Practices for Sharing Your Numbers Files with Colleagues or Clients

Numbers offers several ways to collaborate and share your work with others. Whether you're working on a team project, seeking feedback from colleagues, or sharing a report with clients, Numbers makes it easy to collaborate in real time or share files through various platforms.

How to Share a Numbers File:

1. Click on **File** and select **Share**.
2. You can share via **Mail**, **Messages**, or by generating a **link** to the file, which can be opened on the web.
3. Numbers also supports **iCloud**, allowing you to store your documents in the cloud for easy sharing and access.

Collaborative Features Within Numbers: Comments, Notes, and Real-Time Editing

One of the standout features of Numbers for collaboration is its ability to allow multiple users to edit a document simultaneously in real time. This is perfect for teams that need to work together on the same file, whether for project management, budgeting, or reporting.

- **Comments:** You can add comments to specific cells to ask questions, provide feedback, or make notes without altering the actual data in the cell. To add a comment, right-click on a cell and select **Add Comment**. This is a great way to communicate with collaborators while keeping the document intact.

- **Notes:** Notes are similar to comments, but they can be used to leave more detailed information about a particular piece of data. They are often used for instructions or background context.
- **Real-Time Editing:** If you're working with others on a shared iCloud document, everyone can edit the file at the same time. Changes are immediately visible to all collaborators, making it easy to work together efficiently.

When sharing your Numbers file with others, it's important to ensure that the collaborators have the right permissions. You can set permissions to either allow others to edit or view the document, ensuring that sensitive data is protected.

Advanced Formatting Techniques

Conditional Formatting to Highlight Important Data

Conditional formatting is a powerful feature in Numbers that allows you to automatically change the appearance of data based on certain conditions. This is especially useful for highlighting trends or important values, such as overdue tasks, low stock levels, or high sales figures.

How to Apply Conditional Formatting:

1. Select the range of cells you want to format.
2. Go to the **Format** panel and click on **Conditional Highlighting**.

3. Choose the condition you want to apply, such as "greater than" a certain number or "equal to" a specific value.
4. Select the format style, such as changing the text color or filling the cell with a specific color.

For example, if you are tracking sales performance, you can apply conditional formatting to highlight sales figures that exceed a certain target, making it easy to spot top performers.

Using Themes and Styles for a Polished Look

To ensure your spreadsheet looks professional and well-organized, Numbers offers a variety of pre-designed themes and styles. You can apply these themes to your entire spreadsheet to quickly change the appearance of tables, charts, and text.

How to Apply a Theme:

1. Click on the **Format** button in the toolbar.
2. Choose a theme from the available options. Themes include different font styles, table designs, and color schemes.
3. Apply the theme to your entire spreadsheet, or selectively apply it to specific tables and charts.

Using themes and styles helps give your documents a polished and cohesive look, ensuring that they are not only functional but also aesthetically pleasing.

Practice Tasks

To help you apply the time-saving techniques in this chapter, try these practice tasks:

1. **Use Keyboard Shortcuts:** Practice using the essential keyboard shortcuts listed earlier. Try editing your spreadsheet using only shortcuts to navigate, format, and manipulate data.
2. **Customize a Template:** Open a budgeting template and customize it by adding your own categories and modifying the formulas. Try applying conditional formatting to highlight important spending categories.
3. **Collaborate with Others:** Share a Numbers file with a colleague

and collaborate in real time. Use comments and notes to discuss specific sections of the document.

4. **Apply Advanced Formatting:** Use conditional formatting to highlight key data points in your spreadsheet. Experiment with different styles and themes to enhance the visual appeal of your document.

By mastering these time-saving tips and tricks, you can significantly boost your productivity when working with Numbers. Whether you're using shortcuts to speed up routine tasks, leveraging templates to save time, or collaborating seamlessly with others, these strategies will allow you to complete your projects faster and more effectively.

With practice, these techniques will become second nature, making you a Numbers pro in no time.

Chapter 7: Troubleshooting and Common Issues

Working with spreadsheets can sometimes be frustrating, especially when things don't go as planned. Whether you're dealing with a formula that isn't calculating correctly or experiencing lag when working with large datasets, troubleshooting these issues efficiently is key to maintaining smooth workflows. This chapter will guide you through some of the most common problems users face when using Numbers, along with practical solutions. Additionally, we will discuss how to ensure your spreadsheets are accurate, troubleshoot formatting issues, and improve performance to handle large datasets more effectively. Finally, we will provide some hands-on exercises to help you identify and fix common spreadsheet errors.

Common Problems and Their Solutions

Addressing Common Issues **Like Data Not Calculating or Formulas Not Working**

One of the most common frustrations when working with Numbers (or any spreadsheet application) is when a formula fails to calculate as expected. This problem can arise for several reasons, and knowing how to identify and fix the issue can save you a lot of time.

- **Formula Errors:** Sometimes, formulas don't work because there's a simple typo or a misused function. If your formula is showing an error such as #VALUE!, #REF!, or #DIV/0!, it means there's a problem with your formula.
    - **#VALUE!** typically appears when there's a type mismatch, such as trying to multiply a text value with a number.
    - **#REF!** shows up when a formula references a cell that has been deleted or moved.
    - **#DIV/0!** is displayed when you try to divide by zero, which is not possible mathematically.
- **Solution:** Double-check the formula for typos and ensure that the

referenced cells are correct. Always verify that there's no division by zero or invalid cell references. You can also use the **Formula Auditing** tool to trace which part of the formula might be causing the issue.

- **Cells Not Updating Automatically:** If your formulas are not calculating when you change data in the spreadsheet, it might be due to a setting issue. By default, Numbers should automatically recalculate when changes are made, but if this isn't happening:
  - **Solution:** Check if the spreadsheet is set to manually update formulas. Go to **Numbers Preferences** and ensure that the "Recalculate

automatically" option is selected. If it's set to manual, formulas won't update until you specifically trigger the calculation.

- **Incorrect Data Formatting:** Often, data that doesn't appear as expected is due to formatting errors. For example, numbers might be stored as text, or dates might not be recognized correctly.
  - **Solution:** Check the formatting of the cells. Ensure numbers are formatted as numbers (not text) and dates as dates. You can change the format by selecting the cell and choosing the correct type in the **Format** sidebar.

How to Troubleshoot Formatting and Display Issues

Formatting issues can sometimes make your spreadsheets look messy or difficult to read, which could lead to confusion and errors. Here are a few common formatting and display issues you may encounter, along with their solutions:

- **Cells Not Aligned Correctly:** If your data looks misaligned, it could be due to inconsistent cell padding or a mismatch between the content type and the cell format.
    - **Solution:** Adjust the alignment by selecting the relevant cells, right-clicking, and selecting **Format Cells**. From there, you can adjust the horizontal or

vertical alignment, set text wrapping, or adjust cell padding.
- **Gridlines Missing or Overlapping:** Sometimes, the gridlines might disappear, or there might be an overlap of content making it hard to see the data.
  - **Solution:** Ensure that gridlines are enabled by going to **View** in the top menu and ensuring that **Show Gridlines** is checked. You can also adjust the row height or column width to prevent overlapping content.
- **Inconsistent Fonts or Styles:** If your spreadsheet has inconsistent fonts, sizes, or styles, it can create a jarring reading experience.

- **Solution:** Select the entire sheet or specific cells and apply a consistent font style and size using the **Format** panel. You can also choose a theme to standardize the font style and color scheme across the document.

By identifying and fixing these formatting issues early on, you can ensure that your spreadsheet remains visually organized and easy to read.

Ensuring Accuracy

Double-Checking Formulas and Functions for Errors

Accuracy is paramount when working with spreadsheets, especially when they are being used for important calculations, reports, or business decisions. One small error in a formula or function can lead to incorrect results, which may have serious consequences.

- **Formula Auditing:** Numbers provides a built-in formula auditing feature to help you double-check your formulas. To use this, click on a cell with a formula and look at the **Formula Bar**. If there are any errors or inconsistencies, you can spot them here. You can also use the **Trace Precedents** and **Trace Dependents** tools to see which cells are feeding into the formula or which cells depend on its results.

- **Manual Checking:** Sometimes, manually reviewing your formulas is the best way to ensure their accuracy. Break complex formulas down into smaller parts, checking each one for errors. For example, if you're working with a formula that sums several ranges, check each range individually to ensure the values are correct.

- **Error-Checking Tools:** Numbers also includes tools that can help you spot errors in your formulas. You can set up data validation rules that alert you when a formula returns an invalid result, such as a negative number in a field where only positive values are expected.

How to Audit Your Spreadsheet to Make Sure Everything Is Working Correctly

Auditing a spreadsheet involves thoroughly checking your data, formulas, and overall setup to ensure that everything is functioning as it should. Here are a few steps to perform an audit:

1. **Verify All Formulas:** Go through each formula in your document and ensure that it is working as intended. Use the auditing tools mentioned earlier to trace cells and identify any inconsistencies or errors.
2. **Check for Missing Data:** Sometimes, missing data can cause your formulas to return errors or incorrect values. Scan your dataset for

any blank or missing cells that might affect your results.

3. **Test Your Results:** If you're unsure whether a formula is returning the correct result, test it with known values. For example, if you're calculating a sum, manually add up the numbers in the range and compare the result to the formula's output.

4. **Use a Separate Validation Sheet:** Consider creating a new sheet in your Numbers file dedicated to validation. You can list all the formulas and their expected results, making it easier to track any potential errors.

Improving Performance

Tips for Handling Large Data Sets and Improving File Performance

Spreadsheets can sometimes slow down or even freeze when dealing with large datasets or complex formulas. If you regularly work with large amounts of data in Numbers, improving the performance of your file can significantly reduce frustration and increase efficiency.

- **Limit the Number of Formulas:** Complex formulas can slow down the performance of your spreadsheet, especially when applied to large ranges of data. Try to minimize the number of formulas used or break them into smaller, more manageable sections. Avoid using volatile functions like

NOW() or RAND(), which recalculate every time the sheet is updated.

- **Use Efficient Data Structures:** Instead of creating multiple tables or using large arrays, try to organize your data in a way that reduces the need for complex references. For instance, using smaller tables with clear boundaries can help reduce calculation time.

- **Optimize Charts:** Charts, especially those tied to large datasets, can also impact performance. If you have multiple charts on your sheet, ensure they are optimized to display only the necessary data. Avoid linking charts to entire columns or rows if only a subset of the data is relevant.

Reducing Lag and Optimizing Your Numbers Files

To prevent lag, it's essential to optimize your Numbers files for faster performance. Here are some strategies:

- **Reduce Unnecessary Calculations:** Turn off automatic calculations and switch to manual calculation mode if you're working with a very large dataset. This way, your formulas will only recalculate when you tell Numbers to do so.
- **Use Fewer Cell References:** Excessive cell referencing, especially across different sheets, can slow down performance. Try to keep all relevant data within a single sheet whenever possible.

- **Archive Old Data:** If you're working with a large dataset that includes historical data, consider archiving old records into separate files. This keeps the current working file lighter and faster to navigate.

By following these strategies, you can maintain the performance of your Numbers file even as it grows in size and complexity.

Practice Tasks

To help you improve your troubleshooting and problem-solving skills, try the following exercises:

1. **Fix a Formula Error:** Find a Numbers file with an incorrect

formula and troubleshoot the issue. Use the formula auditing tools to trace errors and fix the issue.

2. **Audit Your Spreadsheet:** Perform a full audit of a spreadsheet, checking for formula errors, missing data, and incorrect formatting. Ensure that all formulas are accurate and that your data is correctly organized.

3. **Optimize a Large Dataset:** Work with a large dataset and try to optimize it for better performance. Reduce unnecessary formulas, adjust your charts, and try archiving older data to improve file responsiveness.

Mastering troubleshooting, ensuring accuracy, and optimizing your Numbers files are essential skills for anyone who works with spreadsheets regularly. By applying the tips and techniques from this chapter, you'll be able to overcome common problems and ensure that your spreadsheets are both functional and efficient. With practice, you'll be able to resolve issues quickly, maintain accuracy, and handle large datasets with ease.

Conclusion

As we come to the end of this guide, it's important to take a moment to reflect on the journey you've undertaken. This book has equipped you with the essential skills and knowledge to not only understand the core functions of Numbers but also to use them efficiently to streamline your daily tasks, enhance your productivity, and tackle more complex projects with ease. Whether you're managing personal finances, running a business, or handling large datasets, the skills you've learned in this book will serve as a solid foundation for mastering Numbers.

Recap of What You've Learned

Throughout the chapters, you have explored the various tools, functions, and capabilities of Numbers, starting with the basics and gradually progressing to more advanced techniques. Here's a quick summary of the key points from each chapter:

- **Chapter 1: Getting Started with Numbers**
  You became familiar with the Numbers interface, learning how to create spreadsheets, navigate between sheets, and enter and organize data. Understanding the basic formatting tools and how to save and share your work was also covered in this chapter.
- **Chapter 2: Functions Demystified**
  You explored built-in functions such as

SUM, AVERAGE, COUNT, and more. These functions simplify calculations and allow you to perform complex tasks quickly. You also learned how to manipulate text and date data, and how to use conditional functions like IF and COUNTIF to automate decisions.

- **Chapter 3: Advanced Functions and Formulas**
This chapter introduced you to more complex formulas and advanced functions like VLOOKUP, HLOOKUP, INDEX, and MATCH, as well as mathematical and financial functions. You gained hands-on experience in combining multiple functions to create powerful formulas for real-world applications.

- **Chapter 4: Mastering Macros in Numbers**

  You learned how to automate repetitive tasks using macros, which can save you significant time. Creating and customizing macros, managing multiple macros, and using them for tasks like data entry and report generation were some of the key takeaways from this chapter.

- **Chapter 5: Organizing and Analyzing Data in Numbers**

  You discovered how to effectively organize and analyze large datasets using tables, charts, sorting, filtering, and Pivot Tables. These skills are crucial for summarizing data and generating meaningful insights.

- **Chapter 6: Time-Saving Tips and Tricks**

  This chapter introduced you to keyboard shortcuts, templates, and advanced formatting techniques. You learned how to use these tools to improve your workflow, collaborate more effectively, and give your spreadsheets a professional appearance.

- **Chapter 7: Troubleshooting and Common Issues**

  You now know how to troubleshoot common problems such as formula errors, formatting issues, and performance problems. Ensuring the accuracy of your data, auditing your work, and optimizing your spreadsheets for performance are now part of your skill set.

As you can see, mastering Numbers involves understanding a wide range of tools, from basic formatting to complex functions, macros, and data analysis techniques. By building on these foundational skills, you are well-equipped to handle most spreadsheet tasks with confidence.

How Mastering Numbers Can Improve Productivity in Both Personal and Professional Settings

Mastering Numbers is not just about learning how to use a software program—it's about significantly improving your productivity in both personal and professional settings. In your personal life, you can apply these skills to better manage your finances, plan projects, or keep track of important dates and events. Whether you're budgeting, analyzing your savings, or organizing your household tasks, Numbers provides the tools to streamline and optimize your processes.

In a professional environment, Numbers allows you to handle complex data analysis, reporting, and presentation tasks with ease. Whether you're managing a small business, working in finance, marketing, or any other field that requires data management, the ability to quickly manipulate and analyze data can help you make informed decisions and save valuable time. By mastering the features of Numbers, you will be able to create more efficient workflows, automate tasks, and present data in a visually compelling way, ultimately boosting your productivity and effectiveness.

Next Steps

Now that you have a solid understanding of the core features and advanced functions of Numbers, it's time to take your skills to the next level. Here are some suggested next steps to continue your learning journey:

- **Practice More Complex Projects:** Start working on more advanced projects that involve complex formulas, data analysis, and automation. The more you apply what you've learned, the more proficient you will become.

- **Explore Advanced Features:** Dive deeper into Numbers by exploring more advanced functions and techniques such as integrating data from other applications, using dynamic ranges, or building advanced financial models.
- **Join Online Communities and Forums:** Participate in online communities like Reddit, Apple Support forums, or specialized Numbers and spreadsheet communities. You can learn from others' experiences, ask questions, and share tips to continue improving.
- **Take Online Courses or Tutorials:** Consider enrolling in online courses or

tutorials to deepen your knowledge of Numbers. Many platforms, like LinkedIn Learning, Udemy, or Coursera, offer courses designed for both beginners and advanced users.

- **Experiment with Different Use Cases:** Try using Numbers for different types of projects—whether it's managing a personal budget, building a business plan, or analyzing large datasets. Each new project will teach you new tips and tricks that you can incorporate into your workflow.

Resources for Further Reading or Courses to Dive Deeper into Numbers

If you're eager to further enhance your skills, here are some resources to consider:

- **Apple's Official Numbers Support** Apple's official support page offers detailed documentation and tutorials to help you master Numbers. It's a great starting point for exploring specific features or troubleshooting problems.
- **Books and eBooks on Numbers** There are many comprehensive books available that dive deep into advanced spreadsheet functions, data analysis techniques, and using Numbers in professional environments. Titles like "Apple Numbers for Dummies" or similar guides can provide more detailed insights.

- **Online Courses:** Platforms like LinkedIn Learning, Udemy, and Coursera offer a variety of online courses on spreadsheet management, including specific courses on Apple Numbers. These courses often feature video tutorials and hands-on exercises to help you progress from beginner to expert.
- **Blogs and Tutorials:** Many spreadsheet and productivity blogs offer in-depth tutorials on using Numbers. Websites like SpreadsheetClass, GCFGlobal, or even personal finance blogs often feature articles or video tutorials on how to use Numbers more effectively.

By continuing to explore and practice, you'll become an even more proficient user of Numbers, and you'll be able to tackle any spreadsheet challenge with ease.

Final Thoughts

Mastering Numbers is a journey, but with the tools and techniques you've learned in this book, you are well on your way to becoming a power user. Whether you are using Numbers for personal tasks, managing a business, or analyzing complex data sets, the skills you've acquired will enable you to streamline your workflows, save time, and improve the quality of your work. Keep practicing, exploring, and applying what you've learned, and soon you'll be able to handle even the most complex spreadsheet tasks effortlessly.

Good luck, and enjoy your continued learning journey with Numbers!

Appendices

A: Keyboard Shortcuts Reference

A quick reference guide to essential shortcuts for Numbers to help you navigate the software more efficiently and streamline your workflow. Mastering these shortcuts will save you time and make using Numbers more intuitive.

General Shortcuts:

- **Cmd + N:** Create a new spreadsheet
- **Cmd + O:** Open an existing spreadsheet
- **Cmd + S:** Save your work

- **Cmd + P:** Print the spreadsheet
- **Cmd + Z:** Undo the previous action
- **Cmd + Shift + Z:** Redo the previous action
- **Cmd + X:** Cut selected content
- **Cmd + C:** Copy selected content
- **Cmd + V:** Paste content
- **Cmd + A:** Select all content
- **Cmd + F:** Find specific content in the spreadsheet
- **Cmd + Shift + F:** Open the format bar
- **Cmd + Option + T:** Add a table to the sheet

Navigation Shortcuts:

- **Cmd + Left Arrow:** Move to the beginning of a row
- **Cmd + Right Arrow:** Move to the end of a row

- **Cmd + Up Arrow:** Move to the top of a column
- **Cmd + Down Arrow:** Move to the bottom of a column
- **Arrow keys:** Move between cells
- **Spacebar:** Scroll through the spreadsheet one row or column at a time

Formatting Shortcuts:

- **Cmd + B:** Bold text
- **Cmd + I:** Italicize text
- **Cmd + U:** Underline text
- **Cmd + T:** Add a new table
- **Cmd + Shift + L:** Align text left
- **Cmd + Shift + C:** Align text center
- **Cmd + Shift + R:** Align text right

Function Shortcuts:

- **Shift + F3:** Open the function editor to enter formulas
- **Cmd + Shift + K:** Insert a hyperlink

B: Function and Formula Cheat Sheet

This cheat sheet is a quick guide to all the essential functions and formulas covered in the book. Use it as a reference when working with Numbers to quickly identify the correct function for your tasks.

Basic Mathematical Functions:

- **SUM(range):** Adds all the numbers in a given range
- **AVERAGE(range):** Calculates the average of numbers in a range

- **COUNT(range):** Counts the number of cells with numbers in a given range
- **MIN(range):** Finds the smallest value in a range
- **MAX(range):** Finds the largest value in a range

Text Functions:

- **CONCATENATE(text1, text2):** Joins two or more pieces of text together
- **LEFT(text, number_of_characters):** Extracts the leftmost characters from a text string
- **RIGHT(text, number_of_characters):** Extracts the rightmost characters from a text string

- **LEN(text):** Counts the number of characters in a text string
- **UPPER(text):** Converts text to uppercase
- **LOWER(text):** Converts text to lowercase
- **TRIM(text):** Removes leading and trailing spaces from a text string

Date Functions:

- **TODAY():** Returns the current date
- **DATE(year, month, day):** Creates a date from individual year, month, and day components
- **YEAR(date):** Extracts the year from a given date
- **MONTH(date):** Extracts the month from a given date

- **DAY(date):** Extracts the day from a given date
- **DAYS(date1, date2):** Calculates the number of days between two dates

Conditional Functions:

- **IF(condition, value_if_true, value_if_false):** Performs a test and returns different values depending on the result
- **COUNTIF(range, criteria):** Counts the number of cells that meet a specified condition
- **SUMIF(range, criteria):** Adds the numbers in a range that meet a specified condition

Lookup Functions:

- **VLOOKUP(value, table, column, [approximate_match]):** Looks for a value in the first column of a range and returns a corresponding value from another column
- **HLOOKUP(value, table, row, [approximate_match]):** Looks for a value in the first row of a range and returns a corresponding value from another row
- **INDEX(array, row, column):** Returns the value of a cell at the intersection of a specified row and column
- **MATCH(lookup_value, lookup_array, [match_type]):** Returns the relative position of an item within a range

Mathematical and Financial Functions:

- **ROUND(number, digits):** Rounds a number to a specified number of digits
- **SQRT(number):** Calculates the square root of a number
- **PMT(rate, nper, pv, [fv], [type]):** Calculates the periodic payment for a loan or investment
- **NPV(rate, value1, [value2], ...):** Calculates the net present value of an investment

C: Sample Templates

Here are links to downloadable templates that you can use for various purposes such as budgeting, project management, and more. These templates are customizable to fit your needs and will help you get started quickly with your own projects.

1. **Personal Budget Template**
   A simple template for managing your monthly income and expenses. Use it to track your spending and plan your savings goals.
2. **Project Management Template**
   A comprehensive template designed to help you manage your projects, from timelines to task management. Customize it for any project you're working on, whether personal or professional.
3. **Invoice Template**
   A customizable invoice template for

freelancers or small business owners. Track your sales, issue professional invoices, and manage payments with ease.

4. **Financial Forecasting Template** Use this template to forecast your future earnings and expenses. It's ideal for both personal budgeting and small business planning.

5. **Sales Tracker Template** Keep track of your sales and monitor progress with this straightforward tracker. Perfect for sales teams, small businesses, and entrepreneurs.

These templates will give you a jumpstart in applying the skills you've learned in this book to real-world tasks, making it easier to organize and analyze data for various purposes.

This concludes the Appendices section, providing you with essential tools, shortcuts, and resources to further enhance your ability to use Numbers effectively. By referring to these cheat sheets and templates as you continue your work, you'll be able to streamline your workflow and complete tasks more efficiently.

Printed in Dunstable, United Kingdom